George McKnight

Firm Ground

Thoughts on Life and Faith

George McKnight

Firm Ground
Thoughts on Life and Faith

ISBN/EAN: 9783337193867

Printed in Europe, USA, Canada, Australia, Japan

Cover: Foto ©Lupo / pixelio.de

More available books at **www.hansebooks.com**

FIRM GROUND.

THOUGHTS

ON

LIFE AND FAITH,

BY

GEORGE McKNIGHT.

PUBLISHED BY THE AUTHOR.

STERLING, N. Y.

CONTENTS.

PART I.

	PAGE.
Prologue to Part I.	9
Gifts	17
Dues	18
Suum Cuique?	19
The Soul's Measure	20
Time's Best Promise	21
All Seek the Good	22
Les Miserables	23
The Arraignment of Chastisement. I.	24
" " " " II.	25
" " " " III.	26
The Inevitable Penance	27
The Ministry of Remorse	28

CONTENTS.

	PAGE
Means of Rescue	29
A Vision of Forgiveness. I.	30
A Vision of Forgiveness. II	31
Rectitude	32
Discernment of Right through Sympathy	33
The Highest Utility	34
Clear Assurance. I.	35
" " II	36
" " III	37
" " IV	38
" " V	39
The Prayer of the Righteous. I.	40
" " " " " II	41
Elihu's Argument. I.	42
" " II	43
" " III	44
The Retrospect	45
Reaching Forth	46
The Estrangement of Happiness. I.	47
" " " " II	48
" " " " III	49
Unhonored Worth	50
"Though naught they may to others be."	51

CONTENTS.

	PAGE.
Perpetual Youth	52
Soul-Food	53
Discernment of the Good and Beautiful	54
"The Soul is dyed by the Thoughts."	55
Kinship	56
Scorn	57
Opportunity	58
Triumph	59
"An Idler in the Land."	60
Consummation	61
Soul-Symmetry	62
In Unison	63
Disinthrallment	64
Live while you Live	65
Memento Mori	66
"Reason thus with Life."	67
Sure Confidence	68
Fearless	69
Death the Renewer	70
Death and Love	71
The Guile of Nature	72
Euthanasia	73

PART II.

	PAGE.
Prologue to Part II	75
Light in Darkness	83
Fidei Fundamentum	84
No Secondary Cause of Love	85
Ubique et Semper. I	86
" " " II	87
'He that formed the eye, shall He not see?"	88
Revealed	89
No Waste of Life	90
The Earliest Need	91
Complaints and Answers. I	92
" " " II	93
" " " III	94
" " " IV	95
The Covenant	96
No Promise Broken	97
Fixed Fate	98
The Birth of Sorrow	99
The Work of Evil	100
The Office of Sorrow	101

	PAGE.
Reconciliation	102
Soul-Light	103
Subjective Truth	104
The Mental Spectrum	105
The Permanence of Truth	106
Crumbled Forms	107
Growths from the Soul	108
The Dimness of History	109
The Test of Truth	110
Recompense of Doubt. I	111
" " " II	112
" " " III	113
The Office of Unbelief	114
Till Clearer Light	115
Diffusive Beauty	116
Formative Beauty	117
The Power of the Ideal	118
Recognition of the Final Cause	119
Partial Readings	120
Light-Gleams	121
The Divine Immanence. I	122
" " " II	123
"The Glory of the Lord shall endure Forever."	124

CONTENTS.

	PAGE.
The Receding Perfect	125
Compensation	126
"Perfect Love casteth out Fear."	127
The Right Eternal	128
The Criterion of Revelation. I	129
" " " " II	130
" " " " III	131

PROLOGUE TO PART I.

SOME record I would leave of trustful hours,
  When livelier sympathy and kindlier mood
Of feeling harmonized the mental powers,
    And seemed to make more clearly understood
    The casual evil and essential good
Of human motives; though full many a deed
    Of sin seemed to require such plentitude
Of pity, reason would to love concede,
Divine compassion must respond to such great need.

Of holy hours, when Duty to incline
    The will to yield a full obedience,
Spake with a tone of majesty divine;
    And, pointing to no other recompense,
    Gave by approving look immediate sense
Of great peculiar favor God bestows
    Upon the just; though lawful consequence
For both the evil and the good dispose
Events, now making glad, now darkening life with woes.

Triumphant hours, when though the changeful look
    Of Fortune darkly frowned, it terrified
Not even the delicate delights that brook
    No hot pursuit, but only will abide
    In souls where love and knowledge are allied,
And, blended, issue forth through gazing eyes;
    Making a vision so serene and wide,
The narrowest horizon will comprise
The beauty of all lands, the glory of all skies.

And of more solemn hours, when Birth and Death
    As Life's successive ministers were viewed; —
One to inspire, one to withdraw the breath,
    As Destiny ordains; and though they stood
    In mutual antithetic attitude
Among the powers obeying Life's control,
    A common end was seen to be pursued
By both, and, to the calmly reasoning soul,
Death evermore appeared the nearest to the goal.

Would that in those serener seasons, when
    The sun of truth seemed with unclouded light
To beam upon me, farther reaching ken
    Had to the eye belonged, or finer sight;
    Or I had stood upon some lofty height
Of learning, where great minds abide alone;
    That looking near or far, I haply might
Have then discovered, and to others shown,
Some precious verities still waiting to be known.

But though the truths I have recorded here
    May be familiar as the flowers that grow
Along the wayside, yet they did appear
    Into my soul immediately to flow
    From their first source ; for I did surely know
Through my own new and clear experience
    Their truthfulness, did feel the warming glow
Imparted to them in that fountain whence
Truths issue and disperse in radiant effluence.

And does not Nature own the wayside flowers ?
    Perchance her rarest beauty is revealed
In dainty petals distant dewy bowers
    Of unfrequented forests have concealed
    From common vision, or the cultured field
Brought forth. Yet could we but discern the true
    And perfect meaning Nature fain would yield
Unto our minds in flowers we daily view,
Their beauty might appear as precious and as new.

And though care-burdened men, day after day,
   Go and return in haste, and give no heed
To blossoms seen so often by the way ;
   Yet haply if a resting traveller, freed
   A season from demands of want and need,
Should note a lowly modest comeliness
   In blooming wayside herbage, then, indeed,
Pure, peaceful thoughts his spirit might possess,
And even some after hours, remembered peace might
   bless.

PART I.

LIFE.

GIFTS.

"Who maketh thee to differ?"

BROTHER, my arm is weaker far than thine;
   And thou, my brother, seest a subtile hue
   Of beauty, overspreading many a view,
Too delicate to thrill such brain as mine.
And yet, O brothers both, by many a sign
   God shows for me as warm love as for you:
   With equal care his light and rain and dew
Cherish the sturdy tree and clinging vine.
Be thou not proud of thy more massive brawn!
   Nor thou, because within thy brain each thread,
   Through which the thought pulsations pass and spread
From cell to cell, has been more tensely drawn!
   God's forces made you what you are, why then
   Should you expect the reverence of men?

DUES.

"Ye are not your own."

AGAINST a soul the accusing angel brought
  Complaint, and said, "The earth has not concealed
  The sweat of one who tilled unpaid thy field—
'T is risen to Heaven!"
                      "He served but as he ought,"
The soul replied. "A suffering wretch besought
  Help of the knowledge God to me revealed,
  And in one hour all his disease was healed;
For this a hundred weeks he duly wrought."
Then from the Throne the words of judgment came:
  "The powers wherewith my servants are endowed
  Are for my service; if, possession-proud,
One for his own behoof or glory claim
  Their use and increase, he will rob his Lord —
  Not his the faithful servant's great reward."

SUUM CUIQUE?

IF finer powers within thy brain inhere,
   Part of mankind's best heritage is placed
   In thy safe keeping. Sad it were to waste
In hard work of the hands a gift so dear.
But shoulds't thou ever from a loftier sphere
   Review thy life — its history retraced
   Through soul-impressions deep and uneffaced —
Within a world where men from year to year
Wrought painfully in body weariness;
   And, while thou shared'st in the pleasant use
   Of what their labor struggled to produce,
Thy own strong arm ne'er felt the irksome stress
   Of that hard toil,— forsooth I fear a trace
   Of shame will overspread thy angel face.

THE SOUL'S MEASURE.

DOST thou of all attainments value those
  Most that enlarge thy soul? and would'st be shown
  A sign, whereby it clearly may be known
How much, from year to year, thy spirit grows?
By as much more as others' joys and woes,
  Through wider sympathy, are made thine own,
  By so much in soul stature hast thou grown.
The bounds of personality that close
Around uncultured spirits narrowly,
  Have been so far extended, and contain
  So much the more of conscious life's domain;
And so much has thy knowledge grown to be
  Like that of clearest souls, whose bounding walls
  Will cast no shadow where the soul-light falls.

TIME'S BEST PROMISE.

O HAPPY thou, whose daily work supplies
   To others joys, that else would never be!
   For thine shall be the happiness and glee
Of many hearts, and thine the goodliest prize
The future showeth to fore-looking eyes:
   For safely are reserved in store for thee
   Occasions for yet nobler charity,—
It may be for sublime self-sacrifice.
The day may come when much of that delight
   Shall in unmingled purity be thine,
   Which fills the souls of messengers divine;
Who, with invisible and silent flight,
   O'er the abodes of mortals have bestrown
   Dear blessings, and forever are unknown.

ALL SEEK THE GOOD.

"And one far off, divine event,
To which the whole creation moves."

DESPISE thou not thy neighbor, though the goal
  Of his endeavors far remote have stood,
  From that which thine have worthily pursued.
The good he gains may be a scanty dole;
Yet 'twould dishonor Him whose high control
  Directs the world, to think that aught but good
  Has been from his omnipotence endued
With power of drawing any human soul.
Though when into men's motives we inquire,
  Sad heedlessness of right we there may find,—
  Negations dark that shock the searching mind,—
Yet whatsoe'er incitement prompts desire
  Is Nature's effort toward the Good to lead,
  But lacking oft just guidance for the deed.

LES MISERABLES.

IF you have pity, O give not the whole
To those whose hopes are dead, though in their dirge
   The moans of present suffering sadly merge:
Spare some to those who yet as seasons roll,
Shall live beneath their base desires' control;
   Whom guilty hopes and secret fears shall urge
   To ceaseless, toilsome efforts, with the scourge
Of discontentment, while the weary soul
No satisfying peace and rest shall find.
   In devious ways they know not, some proceed;
   And see not far nor clearly whither lead
The branching paths they choose: and some, not blind,
   But driven forward by resistless power,
   Approach with conscious steps the torturing hour.

THE ARRAIGNMENT OF CHASTISEMENT.

I.

BEFORE the throne of Justice, Clemency
  In sorely punished man's behalf, arraigned
  Stern Chastisement, and thus her prayer sustained
For lightened penance:

                "Man was never free.
Where'er attraction drew most potently,
  His will has followed — could not have refrained.
  Volition by its own law is constrained;
For the resultant, whatsoe'er it be,
Of all the motives surely must prevail.
  Is't said the will might make itself a source
  Of new created counteracting force?
Nay, that divine prerogative would fail!
  What would incite its use to shun the ends,
  Whereto the sum of all incentives tends?"

THE ARRAIGNMENT OF CHASTISEMENT.

II.

BUT Pity, though so often for man's sake,

With prayers of Clemency her own are blent,

Delayed not then to utter clear dissent.

With wonted tears, unwonted words she spake:

"O cruel kindness! that from men would take

Aught that has power Sin's impulse to prevent,

Though 'twere but selfish fear of punishment!

Such fear's removal from the mind might make

The nearly balanced, oscillating scale

Of a yet guiltless will, sink to the side

Of crime, and all the woes to crime allied.

Then let the penalties of law not fail!

Not mine a wish from sinners to forefend

Correcting Chastisement, their truest friend."

THE ARRAIGNMENT OF CHASTISEMENT.

III.

THEN Justice rendered judgment: " I decree
   A good and needful order of events,
   And Chastisement, my minister, from thence
Derives his duty and authority.
I give to all alike the right to be;
   To all alike the right of self-defence,
   And to prevent unlawful violence
By warding off a coming injury.
And well with all my precepts it consents
   If one, whose unrestrained desires invade
   Another's equal right, himself is made
To feel a hard, deterring consequence.
   If he transgress, his trespass cannot bar
   The other's right,— his own is quenched thus far."

THE INEVITABLE PENANCE.

AGAINST thy penance thou wilt plead in vain
   That laws their full control o'er wills exert:
   The scourging of remorse 'twill not avert!
To this sad knowledge thou shalt soon attain,—
The spirit's sufferings, like the body's pain,
   Can not be measured by the ill-desert
   The test of reason certifies. The hurt
Thy soul will feel, if some base impulse gain
Dominion o'er thy will, and darkly blot
   Thy life,— though much thou longest to make real
   The beauty of a noble life-ideal, —
Will be as keen, though reason doubteth not
   That, in the struggle of that lapsing hour,
   Thy low incentives had resistless power.

THE MINISTRY OF REMORSE.

DOES conscience with most bitter chiding speak?
  The unremitting anguish thou must bear!
  No work of merit, reasoning thought nor prayer
Can cleanse thy life of stains that foully reek.
Is there no remedy? One only seek,—
  Let just and rigorous remorse not dare
  Thy self-abasing penance yet to spare,
Until endurance, lasting, willing, meek,
Imbue thy life with sweet humility.
  O penitent, unwise were thy resort
  To dull, benumbed forgetfulness, to thwart
The painful salutary ministry
  Of one, divinely sent, who hath the power
  To add so dear a grace to thy soul's dower.

MEANS OF RESCUE.

Laws uncreated and omnipotent
  Have shaped thy being, though to sin 'twas made
  So prone. A hard lot was upon thee laid:
But think not 'twas for thee malignly meant!
And though stern Chastisement will not relent
  When aims of thine another's right invade,
  Yet know, the Righteousness supreme, to aid
Thy woful weakness, hath this angel sent.
And if thou art forgiven by God or men,
  Know that a willingness to suffer pain
  And loss, for others' happiness and gain,
Touches thy soul. O, if thou feel it then,
  From sinful aims, that have thy will enslaved,
  Thou may'st by that love-kindling sense be saved.

A VISION OF FORGIVENESS.

I.

IN a sweet dream I viewed, with vision clear,
   A region where departed souls abode.

Bright rivers through the blooming valleys flowed,
And fragrant breezes murmuring soothed the ear;
But all the souls with sin were stained and sere.
   I marvelled and bespake an angel there:
   "Should souls like these abide in this sweet air?
By these pure streams?" The angel answered: "Here
The air is God's own breath of pitying love.
   Forgiveness is diffused unseen therein,
     And gives it balmy sweetness, until sin
Attracting from below, it from above
   Descends as rain and dew; whence are supplied
     These streams, wherein stained souls are purified."

A VISION OF FORGIVENESS.

II.

"BUT must not souls like these, so seared and scarred,
  Insensible to love's warm breath remain?
  And though forgiveness wash away each stain,
Is not their comeliness forever marred?"
I asked. The angel answered: "Naught so hard
  The love of God is shed thereon in vain!
  These souls, though calloused deep by sin and pain,
In this sweet air, made warm by his regard,
At length will feel a softening influence,
  Melting the indurations sin has made.
  Then knowledge of the good must needs pervade
Each soul, and rouse such holy penitence,
  The pardon freely poured in these pure streams
  Will cleanse its stains, and heal its scars and seams."

RECTITUDE.

WHEN hard and painful hindrance has withstood
   Thy course, pursuing Duty's paths that lie
   Distinctly traceable to every eye,
And fair words in thy mind's more troubled mood,
Have promised thy desires undoubted good,
   That far outweighed all ills thou couldst descry
   Borne in the consequence, to justify
One slight departure from thy rectitude;
If still thy moral precepts held control,
   And from the right thou did'st not turn aside,
   Thy human soul has proved itself allied
Most closely to the great majestic Soul
   Of Nature, who will not, for any cause,
   Depart the least from her eternal laws.

DISCERNMENT OF RIGHT THROUGH SYMPATHY.

THE lines of good and evil consequence
   That radiate afar from every deed,
   Thou wilt not clearly see nor justly heed,
Unless endowed with sympathetic sense
Of others' joys and griefs. And only thence
   Arises thy clear knowledge of the need
   Of self-restraint, determined and decreed
By rights of others, for their just defence.
Therefore to make thy moral impulse strong,
   Its aim unfaltering and its scope defined,
   Strive evermore to form within thy mind
The feelings that to other lives belong;
   And, on that stepping stone, rise to the sight
   Of the divine, unchanging laws of right.

THE HIGHEST UTILITY.

THE soul must rise above the selfish care
That so beclouds its vision, ere its view
Of human life, impersonal and true,
And well defining, renders it aware
Of that which is forever good and fair;
Which for itself the right unquestioned claims
To arbitrate between conflicting aims;
Whose seal on Duty's warrant places there
Authority that may not be withstood;
Whose umpirage alone can bring the strife
Between the various elements of life
To that accord which is the highest good;
Whose clear decision seems a high behest
To conscience in the name of God addressed.

CLEAR ASSURANCE.

"If thou workest at that which is before thee, following right reason, seriously, vigorously, calmly, without allowing anything to distract thee, —"

I.

THERE is too much on earth to mourn and rue,
   Too much of body pain in every land,
   And agony of soul, when thou hast scanned
Our human life, to take a mirthful view!
O, soberly and vigorously pursue
   The task required by duty at thy hand:
   Ne'er let a vagrant impulse make demand
Upon endeavors to thy life-work due.
And, trusting God's great purpose doth enclose
   The purposes wherewith his creatures act,
   Accept with equal tolerance each fact,
Whether it aid thy efforts or oppose;
   As unperturbed, if they in failure end,
   As if success their final zeal attend.

CLEAR ASSURANCE.

"But keeping thy divine part pure, as if thou should'st be bound to give it back immedately."

II.

BE mindful always that thou art a child
  Of Nature's hope. The God-like soul, on earth
  Became once more incarnate at thy birth.
Watch well! keep thy divine part undefiled,
Unvexed by envy, calmly reconciled
  To whatsoe'er for thee the years bring forth —
  Disease, toil, penury, unhonored worth.
Keep thy heart's feelings sweet and kind and mild,
Though haughty glances of the unworthy proud
  Cast on thy merit unprovoked disdain;
  And let no selfish purpose with its train
Of troubling cares, even for a day becloud
  The clearness of thy spirit, making dull
  Thy vision of the good and beautiful.

CLEAR ASSURANCE.

"—— If thou holdest to this, expecting nothing and fearing nothing, ——"

III.

NOT as it looks, will be thy coming state.
    It falsely looms to both thy hopes and fears.
    Unwise is he, with prying eye, who peers
'Neath the unturned pages of the book of fate.
Yet whether good or evil hours await
    Thy coming in the far successive years,
    Thou may'st foreknow by that which now appears —
All thou should'st wish to know may'st calculate.
For in thy heart's affections thou can'st see
    What thou becomest as the days go by :
    Think not by skilled device to modify
The strict fulfillment of the high decree,
    That more and more like the sublime or low
    Ideals thou dost cherish, thou shalt grow.

CLEAR ASSURANCE.

"—— But satisfied with thy present activity according to nature, ——"

IV.

SAY not all blessings of thy husbandry
   Are insecure until the groaning wain
   Bears to thy barn the shocks of golden grain!
One harvest was already ripe for thee
While yet unseeded lay thy fallow lea:—
   A harvest that without the summer rain
   May wave abundantly upon the plain,
For souls to reap with glad festivity.
O, tiller, though thy fields yield no increase,
   Because the fleeting clouds their rain refuse,
   Its best reward thy labor need not lose;
For thine may be the sweet contentful peace
   The soul may draw from willing, worthy doing,
   While yet the still eluding end pursuing.

CLEAR ASSURANCE.

"—— And with heroic truth in every word and sound which thou utterest, thou shalt live happy."
Thoughts of M. Aurelius Antoninus.

V.

BUT little harm thy error works to thee,

   Though it continue long, unless, indeed,

   Through self-deception to it thou accede.

Of that beware! Thy lasting hurt 'twill be!

For if in willfulness thou yield the key

   That opes the soul for Truth to enter in,

   Unto her enemy, how can she win

Thenceforth an entrance? O, watch jealously,

If veiled desire persuasively entreat

   Thy reason for the form of an assent,

   To give some fair or subtile argument

Admittance into Truth's peculiar seat!

   Lest treason to the truth, within thy soul,

   Deliver it to falsehood's hard control.

THE PRAYER OF THE RIGHTEOUS.

I.

WHEN thy best efforts fail, when day by day

Thy heart grows sick of hope deferred, and still

New obstacles arise, and omens ill

Threaten thy future, art thou moved to pray?

'Tis well the good incentive to obey.

Pray for a confirmation of thy will

In fealty to duty — to fulfill

All her behests till she commands to stay

The strife, — from unavailing toil to rest.

But with all precious benefits of prayer —

Peace, strengthened purpose, fortitude to bear

Life's evils, thou shalt be most richly blest

If, all thy heart's desires comprised in one,

Thou art content to pray — "THY WILL BE DONE."

THE PRAYER OF THE RIGHTEOUS.

II.

DOST thou desire the Father of us all
   To watch with kindlier providence o'er thee
   Than others? and with importunity
Of strong desires, dost thou upon Him call,
That special influence from heaven may fall
   To bring some lingering joy more speedily?
   Or heal thee of thy grievous malady
When thoughts of early death thy breast appall?
Not mine a wish to lessen aught thy trust
   In power divine. Yet, haply, better aid
   Had been received, if thus thy heart had prayed:
O Father, Thou to all art good and just;
   To help my hope to bloom, myself to live,
   I ask no more than thou to all dost give.

ELIHU'S ARGUMENT.

"If thou art righteous, what givest thou to Him?"

I.

HEAR me, O Job, and heed my words. Although
  Upon the name of the Most High thou call,
  And render truth and righteousness to all,—
Yea, on the worthy poor thy wealth bestow,—
The wind from out the wilderness will blow
  As strongly, though it strike thy dwelling's wall;
  The fire of heaven as fatally will fall,
Although the flocks be thine that graze below.
For thinkest thou thy goodness will augment
  His changeless love? Or, emulous of thine,
  More active grow benevolence divine?
His goodness never sleeps! His powers are sent
  To do their needful tasks, and in each work
  Of seeming waste, conserving efforts lurk.

ELIHU'S ARGUMENT.

"If thou hast sinned, what dost thou against Him?"

II.

IF thou should'st scorn Jehovah's high behest;
   Should'st hear unmoved the orphan's cry of pain;
   And all the toil-won harvest should'st retain,
Though famine sore upon thy plowmen pressed;
The clouds of God above thy fields would rest,
   And shed the early and the latter rain;
   Nor thorns nor weeds would lessen aught the gain
Of barley or of wheat thou gatherest.
Would thy weak wickedness repel the love
   Of the Almighty, when with bounteous hand
   He sows the seed of plenty on thy land?
Behold the skies, how far they stretch above!
   So high is He, howe'er thy sins increase,
   Resentment will not mar His holy peace.

ELIHU'S ARGUMENT.

"For a man like thyself is thy wrong, and for a son of man thy righteousness."

III.

BUT if to all thou render righteously,
  And for all kindly deeds thy loins thou gird,
  On men a benefit will be conferred,
That haply yet may reach far years to be.
And thou shalt treasure in thy memory
  Full many a thankful look and grateful word,—
  Perhaps of some whose hope fled ere they heard
Thy footfalls, bringing rescue sure with thee.
The blessings which the humble poor will breathe
  Upon thee, through each pathway thou shalt trace,
  Will follow thee to thy last resting place.
There, while thou sleepest peacefully beneath,
  Like a low cloud, that outbreathed gratitude
  On thy remembered grave will seem to brood.

THE RETROSPECT.

"Consciousness comes after bliss."

OUR lives are often happier than we know.
   The waters of each stream of life discrete,
   Through all their depth and width with joy are sweet,
Whether they roughly rush or smoothly flow.
Pleasures are ripples bright that seaward go;
   But if the current adverse influence meet,
   The waves upheaved and moved in forced retreat
Against the stream, are surges of life's woe.
And consciousness doth on the surface seem
   To feel both waves and ripples, but it sinks
   Seldom into the depths, nor often drinks
Of the profounder sweetness of the stream:—
   But o'er the past if pensive Memory sweep,
   She sees how bright the current and how deep.

REACHING FORTH.

Though fondly we review both hopes and fears,
  The joys and even the griefs that once we knew,
  We never wish again to live them through.
'Tis not because in that dead past appears
Too much of irksome toil, too many tears;
  Nor yet because of doubt if Memory's view
  Of the delights they held be just and true,
That back to life we would not call those years.
We feel that should our vanished joys revive,
  They would not satisfy to-day's desire.
  Thought dwells on them as earnest of the higher
And more complete delights for which we strive —
  Spurred ever onward by the hope of bliss,
  More satisfying than has been, or is.

THE ESTRANGEMENT OF HAPPINESS.

I.

To neither past nor future giving heed,
   At first the soul enjoyed the present good;
   And Happiness bestowed beatitude
That well sufficed for all the present need.
But soon as Hope came, promising to lead
   To bliss that in the distance dimly viewed,
   With perfect sweetness seemed to be imbued,
And from the unsatisfying wholly freed,
The soul grew eager for the yet ungained;
   And, pressing forward with continual haste,
   Would scarcely linger long enough to taste
The offered joys that present hours contained.
   Thus Happiness was first estranged, aggrieved
   Because her favors were so ill received.

THE ESTRANGEMENT OF HAPPINESS.

II.

THE soul, Hope-led, was prompted to pursue
  Expected joys by Memory, who placed
  In sight her tablets, whereupon were traced
Pictures that seemed of future bliss a view,
Though all their soft, harmonious tints were due
  To the refracted radiance from the past.
  But when the longed-for joys were reached at last,
Harsh Memory, with rude words and untrue,
Chided the present Happiness, complaining
  That all the former sweetness had been changed.
  Thus Happiness was finally estranged
From the pursuing soul,— thenceforth remaining
  Most disappointing and averse forever,
  To those who seek most eagerly her favor.

THE ESTRANGEMENT OF HAPPINESS.

III.

STILL Happiness remembers tenderly

  Her old love for the soul, before the day

  When Hope's eye wounded her with scornful ray,

Ere she had borne the blame of memory.

And sometimes, when with such authority

  Duty commands, the whole will doth obey;

  Or when the visionary thoughts survey

Some lofty phase of Nature's harmony;

And Hope in awe and silent reverence lets

  Pursuit abate, while Memory holds in view

  Only her records of the always true,

All her estrangement Happiness forgets,

  And lavishes upon the soul once more

  Her favor, still more precious than before.

UNHONORED WORTH.

*"All that Nature made thy own
Will like thy shadow follow thee."*

ART slighted and neglected? Dost consume,
  Unloved, the number of thy earthly days?
  Who most deserves the tribute pity pays?
If beauteous, amiable light illume
Thy inner soul, how sad the torpid gloom
  Of any heart, that 'neath the warming rays
  Out-streaming from thy spirit, yet delays
To beautify itself with love's sweet bloom!
Or other minds perhaps do not admire
  Thy natural gifts — do not to thee assign
  The rank among thy peers that should be thine;—
For shame! Insult not Nature! Why require
  Of others confirmation and assent,
  To make thee with her chosen gifts content?

"THOUGH NAUGHT THEY MAY TO OTHERS BE."

IF in these thoughts of mine that now assuage
   The tedium of the toilsome life I live,
   The few who chance to notice should perceive
Nothing their lasting interest to engage,
And quickly cease to turn the farther page,
   It were a shameful thing if I should grieve.

   For if kind Destiny has chosen to give
To other minds, in many a clime and age,
Days brighter than my hours, should I repine?
   And what if by an over-hasty glance
   Some import be not heeded, or, perchance,
Too dim a light upon the pages shine?
   Would I be wronged, even though the wealth I own
   And not the less enjoy, were all unknown?

PERPETUAL YOUTH.

*And ever beautiful and young remains
Whom the divine ambrosia sustains.*

THE days of youth! The days of glad life-gain!
  How bright in retrospection they appear!
  Yet standing in my manhood's stature here,
I ask not Time his fleet hours to refrain.
The joyance of those days may yet remain.
  Fly on swift seasons! Not with grief or fear
  I see your speed increase from year to year;—
The soul may still its bouyant youth retain!
May, if supplied with its celestial food,
  Forever keep so young it will not cease
  To grow in strength, in stature to increase
Through all its days, whate'er their multitude.
  And lo, ambrosia plentifully grows
  On many a field through which thought, culling, goes.

SOUL-FOOD.

"Whence all our spiritual food is brought."

NOT every truth can nourish. It behooves
  A soul to choose its food with care aright,
  If it would grow in the pure spirit's might.
Vainly, with science for its guide, it roves
In search of truth, and clearly parts and proves,
  Unless the verities its guiding light
  Discovers and illumines to its sight,
Augment the objects it admires and loves.
For only when the soul in love extends
  Its sympathy to other life,— acquires
  Similitude to that which it admires,
And thus itself with other being blends,
  It finds its proper, growth-promoting food —
  Experience of the beautiful and good.

DISCERNMENT OF THE GOOD AND BEAUTIFUL.

"And you must love before to you
There will seem worthiness of love."

THAT all the seasons may bring forth for thee
   Soul-food in thought's wide fields, however wise
   And dilligent thy tilth, 'twill not suffice
Unless from selfish care thy mind is free.
The light that to those tender plants shall be
   Most genial is the light of searching eyes
   Long gazing; and the loving heart supplies
The warmth that makes them bloom most fragrantly.
If thou art heedful thus thy land to till,
   Within thy mind's domain there is no field,
   So cold and barren, but has power to yield
Ambrosia, and with joy thy soul to fill.
   And others to thy garnered store will haste,
   To share with thee the sweets that else would waste.

"THE SOUL IS DYED BY THE THOUGHTS."

THE objects whereto the affections move
  Tinge them with their own hues of good and ill;
  And thus related to the soul, instill
Their qualities through all its source of love.
Hence his affection who has naught thereof
  For anything except himself and thee,
  Soon palls the taste with insipidity :|
While his, so large and free it is enough
For thee and all things that are fair and good,
  Comes to thee filled with fragrance taken up
  From every overflowing flower cup
That tints the light of garden, field or wood,
  Wherein his steps in blissful moods have wended,
  When the plant-souls with his in love were blended.

KINSHIP.

"So light yet sure the bond that binds the world."

I FOUND beside a meadow brooklet bright,
  Spring flowers, whose tranquil beauty seemed to give
  Glad answers as to whence and why we live.
With pleased delay I lingered while I might,
Because I thought when they were out of sight,
  No more of joy from them I should receive.
  But now I know absence cannot bereave
Their loveliness of power to give delight,
For still my soul with theirs sweet converse holds,
  Through sense more intimate and blest than seeing;—
  A bond of kindred, that includes all being,
Our lives in conscious union now infolds.
  And O, to me it is enough of bliss
  To know I am, and that such beauty is.

SCORN.

"Which wisdom holds unlawful ever."

IF on a child of Nature thou bestow
   A scornful thought, a grievous punishment
   Is thine; for now no longer evident
Are loving looks Nature was wont to show.
Yet alters not her favor toward thee so;—
   Not really does she thy scorn resent;
   Her heart is too full of divine content
To feel the troubling passions mortals know.
'Tis thou, by harboring unjust disdain
   Within thy selfish bosom, who hast marred
   The beaming tenderness of her regard.
Thy sympathy with her is less, in vain
   Is now each kindly look of hers, each smile
   Of favor thou did'st oft enjoy erewhile.

OPPORTUNITY.

HAS thy pursuit of knowledge been confined
  Within a narrow range by penury,
  And by the hands' hard toil required of thee?
O, sorely tried! But if God had designed
A strong, divinely gifted human mind
  Should in the world appear, and grow to be
  A grand exemplar of humanity,
Perhaps his wisdom, provident and kind,
Seeking a time and place upon the earth,
  Wherein such noble life might grow and bear
  Its perfect fruitage, beautiful and rare,
Would choose and foreordain, tried soul, a birth
  Like that assigned to thee! O, squander not
  The opportunity given in thy lot.

TRIUMPH.

THOUGH hard surroundings, like unsparing foes,
  Against thee have prevailed, a victory
  May yet be thine, and noble life may be
The trophy which thy triumph will disclose.
The world's great prizes thou must leave for those
  Of better fortune! Yield them willingly:
  By so much more thy virtue shall be free
From trammels selfish cares on it impose.
Famed, far off landscapes thou shalt never view!
  Submit: the bliss denied thee do not crave;
  And thy attentive soul a sight may have
Of the omnipresent beautiful and true,
  So clear, 'twill bring thee nearer to thy God,
  Than if thou sought'st his wonders far abroad.

"AN IDLER IN THE LAND."

THE Highest One, I trust, will not despise
  Thy life's oblation, though it be but hours
  Of gratitude and wonder; for in bowers
Of wildest woodland that remotely lies,
Known only to the bee that hath not eyes
  For finer lines and hues, he bids his powers
  Cherish most delicately tinted flowers;
Assuring thus our hearts that he doth prize
For its own sake the beauty, pure and lowly,
  Of fruitless blossoms. Can he value less
  The dearer, unobtrusive comeliness
Of a meek human soul, devout and holy;
  Even if, in bumbleness of life unknown,
  Conspicuous virtues it have never shown?

CONSUMMATION.

"The grand results of Time."

'TWAS needful that with life of low degree
   But slowly rising, long the earth should teem
   Ere man was born; and still the guiding scheme
Seemed not to rest in full maturity.
For Nature since has so assiduously
   Cherished his growth in spirit, it would seem
   That lofty human souls, in her esteem,
Are the best trophies of her husbandry.
And now, as if she neared her final aim,
   She sheds upon them with conspicuous care
   Each fruitful influence, that they may bear
Great and pure thoughts and deeds of noble fame;—
   As if her crowning joy were to transmute
   The sum of Time's results into soul-fruit.

SOUL-SYMMETRY.

Not to win great successes in the fray
  Of right with wrong, nor to create some mould
  Of beauty distant ages shall behold,
The purpose of thy life should choose its way :—
The evidence but not the substance they —
  The blossoms that in due time will unfold :
  But if thy rude haste has the bud unrolled,
Their beauty withers in a summer's day.
Then let the soul in its integrity
  Be nourished well, and if it come to bear
  Such blooming splendor, far-renowned and rare,
That distant eyes flock thitherward to see ;
  Or only leaves, its symmetry shall tell
  Of healthful growth :— 'twill please the Master well.

IN UNISON.

MAY nevermore a selfish wish of mine
  Grow to a deed, unless a greater care
  For others' welfare in the incitement share.
O Nature, let my purposes combine,
Henceforth, in conscious unison with thine,—
  To spread abroad God's gladness and declare
  In living form what is forever fair.
Meekly to labor in thy great design,
O, let my little life be given whole!
  If so, by action or by suffering,
  Joy to my fellow creatures I may bring;
Or, in the lowly likeness of my soul,
  To beautiful creation's countless store
  One form of beauty may be added more.

DISINTHRALLMENT.

Dost strive against thy selfishness in vain ?
  Though grieved and shamed that it so oft should fill
  Thy weary breast with wrangling clamor, still
Do low importunate desires remain
To vex thy peace of soul? Thou shalt attain
  Thy freedom not alone by power of will
  And lofty aspiration; not until
Thou makest others' benefit and gain
The object of thy earnest, strong endeavor.
  And think not even then to disinthrall
  Thy soul from selfish longings once for all,
Thou must again strive on and on forever
  Towards larger liberty. Yet it may be,
  Death will have power at once to set thee free.

LIVE WHILE YOU LIVE.

A VIEW of present life is all thou hast!
  Oblivion's cloud, like a high-reaching wall,
  Conceals thy former being, and a pall
Hangs o'er the gate through which thou'lt soon have passed.
Dost chafe, in these close bounds imprisoned fast?
  Perhaps thy spirit's memory needs, withal,
  Such limits, lest vague dimness should befall
Its records of a life-duration vast.
And artfully thy sight may be confined
  While thou art dwelling on this earthly isle,
  That its exceeding beauty may, the while,
Infuse itself within thy growing mind,
  And fit thee, in some future state sublime,
  Haply, to grasp a wider range of time.

MEMENTO MORI.

LOOK, soul, how swiftly all things onward tend!
　Such universal haste betokens need
　In Destiny's design of pressing speed.
Speed thou, stay not until thou reach the end!
Upon the haste of Time there may depend
　Some far-off good. Thou child of Time, give heed,
　That with a willing heart and ready deed,
To Time's great haste thy dole of speed thou lend!
Though beauteous scenes thy onward steps would stay,
　Press forward toward the Goal that beckons thee —
　The unimagined possibility
Of all the mighty future to assay!
　And when thou drawest near thy hour to die,
　Rejoice that one accomplishment is nigh.

"REASON THUS WITH LIFE."

O, LIFE of mine! I am not well assured,
  That the isolation separating thee
  From boundless being would forever be
Thy highest good. Still to be thus immured
May well be deemed a precious boon, procured
  For none but favorites of Destiny;—
  Even though the walls of personality,
When for a little season they've endured,
Into the Unlimited must surely melt.
  For if thine isolation had not been,
  Sweet life, the many joys of thoughts serene
That have been mine, had not as mine been felt:
  Still, had'st thou been not wholly separate,
  Joys might have been yet more serene and great.

SURE CONFIDENCE.

"When I heard the Earth song,—"
I was no more dismayed.

WHEN I reflect on Nature's mighty past,
  That far transcends the comprehending mind;
  And countless years through which it seems designed
Her unexhausted lifetime yet shall last;
And then with these durations, dim and vast,
  Compare the little space before, behind,
  Wherein my earthly being is confined,
What trivialty on this poor life is cast!—
Unless my soul clings to one truth sublime;
  Whereby its self-assurance still it keeps
  While gazing into those abysmal deeps:—
I'm part of that which was throughout a time
  That reaches far back in eternity,
  And part of that which yet so long shall be.

FEARLESS.

UPON Life's sea how high the billows surge!
   O soul, each bark has need its prow to keep
   Directed well against the wave-fronts steep,
Nor let from that one line its course diverge.
But fearest not when such strong waves shall urge
   Thy fragile skiff, such furious tempests sweep
   Thee, helpless, over the tumultuous deep,
They'll speedily thy being quite submerge?
Nay, my eternal home is that great sea!
   Then why should I, though all unskilled and frail,
   Tremble at coming storms, and fear to sail
The arduous voyage of my destiny?
   I can but sink again, when tempest-spent,
   Into my home and native element.

DEATH THE RENEWER.

'TWAS in far ancient days it did befall :
　The forms of Nature, filling all the space
　Of their abode, had lost their youthful grace ; —
The years were sadly withering great and small.
And when the gods met in their council hall
　To choose out one among their mighty race,
　Who should renew the faded earth's wan face,
None could perform the task among them all, —
So strictly do the laws of Fate restrain
　Each to his proper work — save one alone ;
　Death felt the arduous duty was his own.
Therefore, the sacred synod did ordain,
　And for all time was passed the high decree,
　That Death thenceforth should the Renewer be.

DEATH AND LOVE.

TOWARD Death Love beareth enmity so great,
  From bitter words he can refrain not long,
  Though hushing fears within his breast are strong.
And once Death cried to Jove against such hate:
" I, serving Life most loyally, whom Fate
  Decrees my master, bear a grievous wrong;
  For Love, Life's pensioner, oft joins the throng
Of them that name me but to execrate!"
Then Jove replied, " Was it ne'er told to thee
  How blind Love is? He is Life's careful friend;—
  Thy work in dissolution seems to end,
And so thou seem'st to him Life's enemy.
  For Love, with his dim vision, the return
  Thou renderest unto Life cannot discern."

THE GUILE OF NATURE.

THOU knowest somewhat of Nature's strategems.
  Ofttimes, by strong desire, she moves thy will
  To deeds that profit not thyself, but still
  Are needed to promote her cherished schemes:
  And such thy love of earthly being seems,
    And fear of death's undemonstrated ill.
  'Tis needful that these human ranks we fill
  A little longer here as Nature deems;
So to our weary life vague hope she brings,
  And stills with fear the discontented breast;
  Lest souls become enamored of their rest,
And earth too soon abandoned of her kings;
  Lest dire disorder and calamity
  Befall the plans of highest Destiny

EUTHANASIA.

SEEING our lives by Nature now are led
  In an appointed way so tenderly;
  So often lured by Hope's expectancy;
So seldom driven by scourging pain and dread;
And though by destiny still limited
  Insuperably, our pleasant paths seem free:—
  May we not trust it ever thus shall be?
That when we come the lonely vale to tread,
Leading away into the unknown night,
  Our mother then, kindly persuasive still,
  Shall gently temper the reluctant will?
So, haply, we shall feel a strange delight,
  Even that dreary way to travel o'er,
  And the mysterious realm beyond explore.

PROLOGUE TO PART II.

'TIS needful there should be some stable forms
  Of faith, to give a resting place and stay
To wavering virtue, lest the furious storms
  Of evil impulse bear the soul away.
'Tis needful that on conscious truth we lay
Foundations for the forms of faith, so sure,
  That come the sweeping tempests whence they may,
Resting upon unmoving rock secure,
Those soul-sustaining forms unshaken shall endure.

And well I trust all earnest souls, if each
   Delve in the soil whereon its life has grown,
A sure foundation for their faith may reach.
   The seeming and uncertain are bestrown
   O'er all experience, yet the surely known,
Whose truthfulness all minds may apprehend,
   Lies underneath — firm as the floors of stone
Below earth's varied surface, that extend
The same where valleys sink and stately hills ascend.

O brother, though I seem not well to found
   My joy and confidence in love divine,
Though only few have chosen adjacent ground,
   Whose surface seems to give as doubtful sign
   Of solid rock beneath as this of mine,
Whereon to build belief; although thou trace
   No common stay between my faith and thine,
Connecting while it severs them in space,
Yet deeply they may rest upon the same sure base.

And if the edifice of faith I rear
    Upon foundations that have seemed to me
Both steadfast and secure, to thee appear
    Of scant dimensions, blame not hastily
    The ground whereon it rests. It well may be
If I had delved more widely, and laid bare
    A broader underlying certainty,
A risen structure would have stood even there,
As high as thou hast built — as stately and as fair.

Yet, brother, scorn not the abode wherein
    My soul with peace and comfort doth reside;
For it hath spacious, lightsome rooms within:
    Hath one with outlook unobscured and wide,
    Whereinto shine the stars on every side;
Where hope finds refuge when by fear sore pressed.
    For signs of Highest Goodness, verified
By clear responses heard within the breast,
Have builded for my soul a bower of holy rest.

Hath one, that often to the externally
    Beholding, shows a gloomy look within;
For evidence of sad necessity
    Requiring conflict, suffering and sin,
    And all the ills that are, or e'er have been
Hath reared its walls: yet if my spirit choose
    Therein to dwell awhile, its sight can win,
Of human life and ruling laws, such views
As with contentful peace the feeling thought infuse.

It hath another, whose transparent sides
    Consist of clear persuasions that all light
Has come from heaven. Within it Doubt abides,
    And for all outward radiance claims a right
    To enter — both the beautiful and bright
And that which clouds reflect of sombre hue.
    Yet oft my soul there stays the livelong night:
For in the darksome hours 'tis only through
Clear, crystal walls can pass gleams of the fair and true.

And one, whose consecrated space no sound
  But thanksgiving and adoration knows.
Confirmed beliefs in Mind that hath no bound,
  And in all being lives and rules, compose
  The lasting structure of its walls that rose
As if by power of music; when the sign
  Of conscious purpose, Nature often shows,
Did with the reasoning consciousness combine
To form a silent chord — faith in a Thought Divine.

PART II.

FAITH.

LIGHT IN DARKNESS.

> "Though Nature, red in tooth and claw,
> With ravin shrieked against his creed."

How oft, when seamen on a wreck from whence
   The foaming billows soon must sweep them, plead
   With Heaven for help in that drear hour of need,
The storm roars on, none of its rage relents!
Such harsh succession of the earth's events,
   And early deaths whereof there seems no heed
   In Nature's heart, might make us doubt, indeed,
If aught but selfish strife of the elements,
The ordinations of the world controls!
   Yet in the Uncreated there must be
   A source of predetermined tendency
Which shapes at least a few sweet human souls —
   Of goodness and of beauty types serene —
   Else one my heart has loved would ne'er have been.

FIDEI FUNDAMENTUM.

"If I but remember only,
Such as these have lived and died."

MY soul's grief can not rightfully atone
  Even for one hour of an ungrateful mood.
  Our blessings lay a debt of gratitude
Upon us, that remains when they have flown.
Sweet, disembodied soul! O, you have shown,
  In the unselfish aims your life pursued,
  So clear an evidence that God is good,
My trust in Him no faltering should have known;
Nor can I ever with just reason fear
  As one who feels no firm ground for his faith;
  Even though you were not saved from early death!
Even though I never more on earth shall hear
  The soft tones of your words so true and wise,
  Nor see the tender glow of your dear eyes.

NO SECONDARY CAUSE OF LOVE.

NO chance from selfish motives could compose
　The unselfish goodness we have known to be.
　That which in human hearts we sometimes see,
In Nature's heart pure goodness doth disclose.
Search ye its forming cause? Your science throws
　In vain its light upon that mystery.
　Thou Cause beyond our knowledge! thanks to thee
For all unselfish love life ever shows: —
For every action of self sacrifice,
　Country or race or kindred to defend;
　For every kindly thought of friend for friend
That e'er was told by looks of meeting eyes,
　Whereby our doubting minds may clearly prove
　That in thy Being is a source of love.

UBIQUE ET SEMPER.

I.

LOVE that regards not self we daily feel!
  Rejoice my soul, that thou such love dost know;
  And should the wise, defining clearly, show
The power of love, with its true warmth and zeal,
In many an instinct lower lives reveal,
  Rejoice no less. But on no aim bestow
  The name of love unless it outward go —
Abandon self to work another's weal.
O spirit of Love, dost thou indeed pervade
  All the degrees of Being? All the more
  Will I thy omnipresent power adore!
Although thy function in each lower grade
  Dim knowledge to our minds of thee imparts,
  "Till thou revealest thyself in human hearts.

UBIQUE ET SEMPER.

II.

SHOW me that lower instincts have ascended
During vast time in slow gradation due,
'Till to the height of human love they grew!
Yea, even that these arose from force expended
In orbits of primeval atoms blended
In the old chaos! Joyful were such view
Of the unselfish impulse, active through
The world's vast former lifetime, and extended
Beyond into eternity foregone.
If ancient atom-pulses have become
Through favoring concurrence, in their sum,
Motives that to all kindly deeds lead on
The human soul, doubt not they always strove
In the direction, with the aim of love.

"HE THAT FORMED THE EYE SHALL HE NOT SEE?"

IF love has been created, if it flows
   Not forth immediately from the Divine;
   If to bring aught to pass along some line
Of His great scheme, it pleased God to compose
Love out of elements that ne'er disclose
   The power and aim of love till they combine,
   The inward thought that must be, ere design
To outward, realized existence grows,
Would still support our trust that God is good.
   Though He who formed the eye see not with eyes,
   Yet must the earliest purpose to devise
Sight for the yet unseeing, have pursued,
     As final object, that which adumbrated
     The vision then existing, uncreated.

REVEALED.

O, JUDGE not Nature by the mantle cold
That wraps the wintry earth and all its graves,
Nor by the summer landscape as it waves
Beneath the breeze. To thee was never told
The meaning those external views infold;
In vain thy soul with theirs communion craves.
But if the power of life to thee yet saves
Dear human fellowship, and thou canst hold
Within thy heart the joys and griefs that swell
Another's heart, whene'er with blest surprise
Deeply-illumined, softly-glowing eyes
Meet with thy own, thou understandest well
What Nature then reveals to thee. O, rest
Thy thought of her on what thou knowest best.

NO WASTE OF LIFE.

*And early deaths whereof there seems no heed
In Nature's heart,—*

HEAR what self-vindicating Nature saith:—
"In hymeneal songs I tell my mirth.
My yearning endeth in each new life's birth
That fullness of my love inheriteth.
My hardest strife is to prolong the breath
Of helpless young, in danger, cold and dearth.
My tears in parents' eyes bedew the earth
Beside the monuments of early death.
I, heedless that so many must forego
Life's sweetness after one short moment's taste?
Each brief existence proves I will not waste
One drop of precious life, but will bestow
On each, with equal, unremitting care,
Its least and greatest law-appointed share."

THE EARLIEST NEED.

*"That self might be annulled—its bondage prove
The fetters of a dream opposed to love."*

MOURN that man's soul is selfish, but defame
   Not Nature. Thy regrets 't will soothe to heed
   His spirit's adolescence. Thou 'lt concede
One want may his first efforts justly claim.
To grow must needs be the young soul's first aim,
   Yea, duty! and the motives which this need
   Begets, and rears into accomplished deed,
Though selfish, do not all deserve thy blame.
When such maturity the soul attains,
   That care of self may cease, then it extends
   Its sympathy to other lives, and blends
Its joy with theirs, its sorrow with their pains;
   And finds through consciousness of brotherhood
   Its own desire sufficed by others' good.

COMPLAINTS AND ANSWERS.

I.

WHEREFORE, O Nature, thy excessive zeal?
　Thy aims are doubtless right but oft the deed
　Of time and place appears to take no heed,
And therefore not to reach the general weal.
'Tis not that thou should'st less profusely deal:—
　We chide thee not because the ripened seed
　So oft surpasses all apparent need—
Such care thou seemest for thy types to feel.
But when thou seest death invade our life,
　'Gainst his approach thou dost protest through pain,
　Sometimes prevailing, and sometimes in vain:
O why, when hope remains not in the strife,
　Dost thou prolong thy ineffectual plea
　Of agony, for life that cannot be?

COMPLAINTS AND ANSWERS.

II.

THINK not, my children, that the spring's bare plain
  Alone incites my care of seeds,— know ye,
  The very germs of life are dear to me,
Although their hope of growth they ne'er attain.
And call not *fruitless pangs* my protest vain
  Against the near destroying power I see
  Approach a life I love too tenderly.
Behold the struggling life itself is pain !
And can ye find it in your hearts to blame
  My ceaseless love, and charge it with excess,
  Because when life's low fire grows less and less,
And now burns only with a flickering flame,
  I will not quench it, nor the faintest spark
  That lingers yet awhile ere all is dark ?

COMPLAINTS AND ANSWERS.

III.

THE best of human rulers oft forego
   A wonted law-enforcement, if it lead
   To grievous hardship. Laws by thee decreed,
O Sovereign Nature, are not tempered so
By mercy, but alike through joy and woe
   Unanswering, unrelenting, still proceed!
   Forsooth of fixed succession there is need,
That thinking beings may their future know.
Yet such slight swerving as would oft avert
   Unmeasured anguish, scarce could make us lose
   Faith in our prescience. Still thou dost refuse.
Does order so much more control exert
   In thy heart than in ours — or so much less
   The care of sentient creature's happiness?

COMPLAINTS AND ANSWERS.

IV.

YE well may grieve, O children, if it seem
  My constancy to order e'er impedes
  The granting of one boon for which love pleads!
Within my heart the longing is supreme
To give and cherish life, and none will deem
  The love of mere unloving order leads
  My just, undeviating course, who heeds
The vast repleteness of the world's life-scheme.
Of life, real and potential, know ye well,
  The universe is full! My pulses waste
  No intermediate efforts while they haste
From life to life its progress to impel.
  Where'er my law-directed purpose tends,
  The means through which it passes all are ends.

THE COVENANT.

THE properties of the elements, if scanned
  When thought is clearest, seem the seal extant
  Of an inviolate, solemn covenant,
Wherein has been with plain distinctness planned
A scheme of bounty that unchanged shall stand.
  Omnipotence is firmly bound to grant
  Each promised favor, which the feeblest want,
Assured of full performance, may demand.
Each particle of being, though but dust,
  That flies and whirls according to the laws
  Of outward and of inward forces, draws
Its proper share in the allotment just
  Of help divine, toward the one perfect end
  Whither created beings strive and tend.

NO PROMISE BROKEN.

JUSTICE of God, O most impartially
  Thou judgest! Though we scarce can bear the light,
  Of heavenly emanations, pure and bright,
As thy divine, transcendent equity.
The lowest worm will ne'er be wronged by thee;
  Though the denial to so mean a wight
  Of some small portion of its lawful right,
Would save a noble life from agony,
And grant a boon besought with urgent prayer.
  Thy sentence is that promises divine,
  Which Nature's laws promulgate and define,
Shall not to one be broken, though its share
  Of favor be so small, 't would seem not hard
  So low and mean a thing to disregard.

FIXED FATE.

AMONG the sons of God the Accuser came
 And said : " Your willing virtue is not free :
 That which ye are doth lay necessity
Upon your choice — ye must and will the same.
The Eternal Will cannot exemption claim
 From laws the Eternal Being doth decree :
 Effect and cause are linked unchangeably,
Constructing Destiny's unyielding frame."
Then answered he, the Clearly Seeing called :
 " True, O Accuser, as thy words have shown,
 The effect that is was possible alone !
But thinkest thou our hearts can be appalled
 By that wherein we find assurance blest ?
 The Possible is one, since 't is the best."

THE BIRTH OF SORROW.

WHEN Sorrow first appeared in Heaven of yore,
  The angels by the voice of Fame beguiled,
  Believed he sprang from God's unreconciled
Resentment toward some wrong that vexed him sore.
But strange it seemed — they marvelled more and more —
  That one of mien so meek, and look so mild,
  Should be of such stern parentage the child;
Till heavenly Truth her tidings to them bore:
" This beauteous stranger seraph whom ye see,
  Is offspring of that Hierarch benign,
  Who reconciles in unison divine,
The perfect peace of present Deity
  And strifes through which Creation's work goes on,—
  Of God's great Patience ye behold the son."

THE WORK OF EVIL.

IN the great Hierarchy of the skies
   The seat of Harmony is next the Throne,
   To the angels, times and places to make known
Wherein obedient zeal to act should rise.
Now Satan's fall of old was in this wise:
   Once, when desire that just before had flown
   Warm from the Eternal Heart, throbbed in his own,
With Harmony not waiting to advise,
He flew in haste the prompting pulse to obey.
   Thus he estranged the highest harmony;
   And then not knowing how to make agree,
His works with Nature's wants, became the prey
   Of unadapted impulse,— and he still,
   Striving to do the good, does only ill.

THE OFFICE OF SORROW.

BETWEEN the world-directing Harmony
   And Evil — who 't is said in Heaven once bore
   A name remembered on the earth no more —
Estrangement grew to such high enmity,
The peace of Heaven was brought in jeopardy, —
   Contentious thoughts that ne'er were known before
   Vexing celestial bosoms o'er and o'er!
Still the Supreme chose not by stern decree
To exercise His high arbitrament;
   But summoning a seraph from among
   His waiting messengers, one fair and young,
Sorrow by name, him graciously he sent,
   On Evil's restless ardor to impose
   Restraining guidance of experienced woes.

RECONCILIATION.

Although at first impetuous Evil spurns
  Sorrow's restraints, they grow in strength until
  The purpose of their being they fulfill,
And Harmony no more offence discerns.
But Evil with unlessened longing yearns -
  Toward the divine activity ; and still,
  When pulses of divine incitement thrill
His being, with intemperate zeal he burns.
Therefore must constant Sorrow yet restrain
  His zealous ardor, that his deeds may be
  Acceptable to highest Harmony.
And thus it seems it ever shall remain : —
  As moderating guardian till the end,
  Sorrow on Evil closely shall attend.

SOUL-LIGHT.

HAVE reverent faith in every spirit's light!
  Doubt not 't is from that sun whose effluence
  Diffuseth widely God's intelligence —
The faint reflections from the clouds of night,
No less than day's warm beams, direct and bright.
  Have faith in every spirit's inner sense
  To feel the sameness and the difference
Of light-impressions made upon its sight.
But the results of definition, doubt,
  That limits by our knowledge outward things.
  This is the source whence all our error springs;
For of the mystic universe without,
  We know the nearest part does not reflect
  Its perfect image to the intellect.

SUBJECTIVE TRUTH.

WHEN of the elements which sense supplies,
   Ideas are through definition wrought,
   These then become the molecules of thought
That into creeds and dogmas crystallize.
And all creeds that spontaneously arise
   Are shaped by Nature's forming hand,— in naught
   Are crystal gems to more perfection brought,
With all the exactness of their symmetries.
But if beliefs are shaped unerringly
   By Nature, are they to her facts untrue?
   They are not so save to an outer view.
With outward facts they all may disagree,
   But with the inward still they harmonize —
   True always to the minds wherein they rise.

THE MENTAL SPECTRUM.

OF the reflected rays of soul-light, few
  From nearest objects reach the intellect;
  And formed beliefs within the mind deflect
And part them variously while passing through,—
Making the images they cast not true
  To outward things. Yet 'tis by this defect
  Of mind-transparency that we detect
Most beauteous beams, else hidden from our view.
'Tis thus the falling rain drops, half opaque,
  The clear, uncolored sunbeam decompose;
  Yet the refracted light which through them flows
Is that which God selects, when he would make
  A sign to gladden every creature's eye,
  And sets his rainbow in the evening sky.

THE PERMANENCE OF TRUTH.

"All the forms are fugitive,
But the substances survive."

OUR creeds of living essence of the mind
   Consist, of conscious life-experience,
   Which by the lights and shades of evidence
Has into formed ideas been defined.
And though full many a creed may have declined
   Within our souls, they failed not wholly thence:
   Their substance shares the spirit's permanence
Though to decay their forms have been consigned.
And should the essence of the mind remain
   Fixed in one form, with no progressive change?
   Through higher, fairer ranks no longer range
The unfulfilled Ideal to attain?
   Nature not always will permit to hold
   Her liveliest substance in one hardened mould.

CRUMBLED FORMS.

WHEN we look backward to the early rise
Of human thought — to Faith's far distant youth,
We see in old beliefs, strange and uncouth,
Much that all earnest souls forever prize,
Though many a present creed we quite despise;
Because form-crumbling years have freed, forsooth,
Those ancient faiths from falsehood, while their truth,
Substantial, still remains beneath our eyes.
But loving souls are strengthened by discerning
The truth in every faith on which they brood;
Long ere its form, perhaps unfit and rude,
And hardened in the flames of zeal still burning,
The crumbling power of lapsing time has felt;
For by their softening warmth all forms they melt.

GROWTHS FROM THE SOUL.

'TIS pleasant wending peacefully and slow
   Among the creeds, in thought's warm, still retreat,
   To note their outward contrasts, and to greet
The inward harmonies of soul they show.
The roots of all strike deeply, far below
   In spirit-substance. Rising, they may meet
   Misshaping influence, but life-sap sweet
They draw from out the soil whereon they grow.
And throughout all that wondrous wilderness,
   From every bough a spirit fragrance drips,
   And fruit hangs down even to the hungry lips
Of him who through the forest dares to press.
   And underneath each lofty growth are found
   Sweet flowers of feeling, covering all the ground.

THE DIMNESS OF HISTORY.

FOR me, dense ignorance beclouds past time,
  Except the little space that memory clears;
  Save when my ear, with eager listening, hears
Wise men, whom Destiny permits to climb
Earth's speculative heights, serene, sublime;
  As they narrate how to their sight appears
  The far extending retrospect of years —
Even far away toward human story's prime.
But, ah me, they report so variously!
  And no fit umpire, I, with measured line
  From point to point those objects to define,
Which they upon the heights but darkly see!
  I only feel in this one faith secure,—
  Then were, as now, the just and good and pure.

THE TEST OF TRUTH.

IF ye have precious truths that yet remain
   Unknown to me, O teach me them! Each way
   Into my soul I open wide, that they
May enter straightway and belief constrain.
But urge not fear of loss nor hope of gain
   To rouse my will, and move it to essay
   To shape my soul's belief, or tinge one ray
Of Nature's light! All willful faith must pain
The Genius of true Faith, who asks assent,
   Not even to dearest truths, until the hour
   Arrives of their belief-compelling power;
In order that the force they will have spent
   In wrestling with our unbelief, at length
   May be transformed into believing strength.

RECOMPENSE OF DOUBT.

"There is more faith in honest doubt,
Believe me, than in half your creeds."

I.

AN angel whose delight is to dispense

God's truth, thus to a prophet gave command:

"Take now this truth, and going through the land

Teach it in form that fits the intelligence

Of them that hear;—a blessed consequence

Succeeds true faith." * * * But when the prophet scanned

His finished work, and saw a blessing hand

Distribute faith's rewards, he took offence.

For some souls who appeared to have full well

Accepted all the message he declared

From Heaven, had in the heavenly blessing shared

Even less than others, who, most strange to tell,

In doubt, on farther scrutiny intent,

Still to a truth of God delayed assent.

RECOMPENSE OF DOUBT.

II.

THE prophet to the angel then addressed
    Complaining words: "With credence undelayed
    These willingly accepted all I said.
Why are not they conspicuously blessed?"
And thus the angel answered: "Though professed
    So promptly, yet this faith does not pervade
    Their being,— only on the surface laid
And lightly by thy power thereon impressed.
The doctrine thou hast offered them they take
    With languid scrutiny, assent inert.
    Not thus can truth its conquering force exert!
And only souls that full resistance make,
    Are, when convinced, assimilated well
    Unto the truth. Let it belief compel!"

RECOMPENSE OF DOUBT.

III.

"Thou Bearer of God's truth to men, O why
  Have these, who yet have no belief confessed,
  Received of faith's rewards the most and best?"
"They have believed," the angel made reply,
" And now in words of thine new proof descry,
  That every verity, in form expressed
  Befitting well the intelligence addressed,
And with clear light illumined to the eye,
Has power to win of souls their due assent.
  This, realized by them in all its force,
  Has of their heavenly blessing been the source;—
By faith in truth and in the soul content
  To wait, serenely calm, the coming hour
  Of truth's authentic, soul-convincing power."

THE OFFICE OF UNBELIEF.

TRUTH has prevailing power 'gainst all reply,
  The due effect whereof she cannot lose,
  Except when arrogant beliefs refuse
To let the reason scan and testify.
But Unbelief will be thy firm ally,
  O Truth, and will remain, if her thou choose,
  Most faithful, though defaming tongues accuse
Her faithfulness, and say she will deny
Thy right to enter souls! She does but strive
  To keep thy beautiful abodes unmarred
  By lawless occupancy, and to guard
Against wrong ingress until thou arrive;
  And with a voice of unmistaken tone,
  Demand and gain entrance into thine own.

TILL CLEARER LIGHT.

ALTHOUGH we may not choose nor hold a creed
   Because the heart's strong yearning it contents,
   Yet whatsoe'er belief with fact consents,
And satisfies within the soul the need
Of harmony,— giving a clew to lead
   The unperplexed, assured intelligence
   Through all the mazes of experience,
Reason may to our lives strong want concede.
For 'tis the work of Truth to reconcile
   All discords; and whatever in her name
   Fulfills her arduous function, well may claim
Of loyal souls to be received, meanwhile,
   Till superseded by an embassy
   Of higher grade in Truth's vicegerency.

DIFFUSIVE BEAUTY.

THE presence of the beautiful ye know
   By one sure sign, in only one blest hour;
   'T is only when ye feel your souls' own dower
Of beauty larger, more contentful, grow.
And all its outward sway doth beauty owe
   Unto its widely self-diffusing power,
   That radiates from the petals of a flower,
From lines and angles of a flake of snow;
That makes the stars shed peace serene and great
   On troubled minds through upward looking eyes;
   One noble action of self-sacrifice
The daily lives of millions elevate;
   And clear, accordant songs of souls sublime
   Echo from kindred souls through endless time.

FORMATIVE BEAUTY.

WHENE'ER the atoms into forms combine,
  The grouping, shaping forces seem to owe
  Allegiance to the beautiful, and show
Beauty has power to mould and to define.
Its blessed presence seems a potent sign
  Which e'en obdurate elements well know;
  Toward it alone will Nature's favors flow,
Even with its measure metes the Grace divine.
For when, attent, the beautiful we view,
  And radiant beauty enters through the sight,
  The soul is filled with hope and deep delight;
As if its being were assured anew;—
  As if the right to be had been bestowed
  Only where Beauty maketh its abode.

THE POWER OF THE IDEAL.

THE forms that are do not alone decide
   The course of plastic Nature: rights of these
   Limit the power of onward tendencies;
But forms to be, the shaping effort guide.
Mark what the mental vision verified
   By reason, in rebounding bodies sees!
   When equipoise of clashing energies
Is reached, the undriven atoms backward glide —
A form that was and is not, but shall be,
   Determining the swift, exact recoil.
   And likewise witnesseth the artist's toil,
That still unfashioned forms most potently
   Arouse and rule efforts to make them real,
   Through Beauty's power, efficient though ideal.

RECOGNITION OF THE FINAL CAUSE.

NOT ours to know the purposes that guide
   The aims of Nature, but when they are brought
   Within our souls, we then are clearly taught
The power of final causes to decide
The *modes* wherein the energies abide.
   Belief therein we need to build our thought
   Of every natural process, and 'tis wrought
Deep in all theories our minds have tried.
We need it realized forevermore
   Full clearly, with all cogency of proof
   Through varied instance, for the heart's behoof:
For what have we to love or to adore,
   Unless we feel wise purpose justly reigns
   Over a world of strifes and toils and pains.

PARTIAL READINGS.

Though the great Scroll wherein have been outlined
  By Nature, thoughts of God, deep and immense,
  We can not read, yet gleams of meaning thence
At times shine on us, clear, distinct, defined.
Hence comes assurance that the human mind
  Though weak in reason, and obtuse in sense,
  Still owns a share of that intelligence
Whereby the great World-builder has designed
The wondrous plans which Nature's works disclose.
  A child who scans the philosophic page
  Of some profoundly meditative sage,
May see familiar phrases,— then he knows
  That his own simple thoughts and childish lore
  Are part of the great scholar's mental store.

LIGHT-GLEAMS.

GOD'S glory, lest it blind our human sight,
  Hath been behind material forms concealed;
  Yet to our eyes brief glimpses are revealed
Of radiance we must deem divinely bright.
For hast thou not had moments when such light
  Has gleamed upon thy soul, 't was forced to yield
  It worship? In a throng or lonely field,
'Mid day's effulgence or the gloom of night,
When gazing on a landscape, star or cloud,
  Strong rapture seized thee, and before a view
  Of the forever Beautiful and True,
In reverence profound thy spirit bowed
  For one brief moment; then the vision passed.
  O, that such gleams of the divine would last!

THE DIVINE IMMANENCE.

"All are but parts of one stupendous whole,
Whose body Nature is, and God the soul."

I.

GOD from the world distinguish,— from the great
  But known Effect, the unknown greater Cause!
  From aught our minds conceive, that which but awes
Our souls with thoughts that past their bounds dilate.
But call these twain not wholly separate.
  Confess that every natural process draws
  Its moving power through channels, which as laws
Within the heart of God originate.
And may there not be nerves which from the seat
  Of the Divine Intelligence arise
  And reach the world's remotest boundaries?
Unfelt are these by us,— they do not beat
  Like arteries of Law even to their ends
  When the great Heart its life-pulsations sends.

THE DIVINE IMMANENCE.

*"If we could see and hear,
The vision, were it not He?"*

II.

NO doubt a wise philosopher was he
Who called the Universe "Thought petrified;"
But does a whole truth in his words abide?
Perchance the Thought Divine not really
Is petrified: all this solidity
   May be my sense of being, that outside
   My own continues, and so unallied,
It but resists,— yields me no sympathy.
But if the hills and valleys are to One,
   O soul of mine, as now thy subtile essence
   Is unto me, through a pervading presence,
And through the inner life's experience known,
   To Him their substance may appear as free
   From stony hardness, even as thine to me!

"THE GLORY OF THE LORD SHALL ENDURE FOREVER."

THE forces that prevail eternally,
   And those that seem to quickly vanish hence,
   Are emanations from Omnipotence
Of self-conserving, ceaseless energy.
And whatso in the changeless entity
   Of God originates, partaketh thence
   Of the divine, essential permanence :—
Whatever is because He is, shall be.
O, then to strengthen trust, thyself assure,
   In every fearful, every doubting mood,
   From God came forth the Beautiful and Good ;
And as the Eternal Glory shall endure,
   They in His changelessness shall still abide
   Unwasted, mid destruction far and wide.

THE RECEDING PERFECT.

"NO man may look upon my face and live!"
'Tis well he veils perfection from our sight;
And if because of visions clear and bright,
Which raptured souls in ecstacy achieve,
They deem assuredly that they perceive
  A perfect type of the Eternal Beauty —
  Truth absolute, the final Goal of Duty —
That day they suffer death without reprieve!
Since one activity within the mind,
  Through which its highest life is manifest —
  One effort toward the unattained Best,
Must then its final check and limit find:
  'T is satisfied, it makes no farther quest,
  It can but sink to death's unending rest!

COMPENSATION.

GOD asks from creatures for his plenitude
  Of goodness, no return. Without the hire
  Of prayer or praise or love, till they expire
He feeds the teeming earth's unthankful brood.
That each demand shall with the general good
  Of all consist, his justice must require;
  And to his yearning bounty, such desire
Ascends a grateful offering, like food
To weary, fainting men whom famine gnaws.
  The creature need affords a counterpart
  To the outflowing of the Mighty Heart.
Recurrent stream of love! supply it draws
  From wants of all created life, and pours
  Replenishment into love's primal source.

"PERFECT LOVE CASTETH OUT FEAR."

FEAR thou a creature with self-guarding fear.
   Too far from thee for sympathy, the ill
   Thou offerest him he may return, until
The hard requital brings thee penance drear.
But fear not so the One to thee so near
   His being doth include thy own — His will
   Rewilling thy volitions, doth fulfill
Their aims through powers that not in thine inhere.
And O, beware lest thy distrusting doubt
   Dishonor Love divine, and the attribute
   Of narrow finitude to it impute
By deeming any soul can be without
   Its blest embrace. At once each fear reprove
   And hush by faith in all-including love.

THE RIGHT ETERNAL.

*"The wrong that pains my soul below,
I dare not throne above."*

IF any, as an advocate who pleads
  Religion's cause, shall to mankind proclaim
  The rule and test of right is not the same
For motives whence a human act proceeds,
And purposes of God's great sovereign deeds,—
  That right, forsooth, by God's command became,
  Beware of the false prophet! In the name
Of Faith's defender, he avers what needs
Must the foundation of all faith remove.
  For what supports even your most holy trust
  That all is well, and will be with the just,
If your clear intuitions do not prove
  The laws of right which pure souls apprehend,
  Unchanged, throughout all time and space extend.

THE CRITERION OF REVELATION.

I.

THUS spake Elisha to the Shunamite:
"The angel of the Lord, with voice to dread,
Has bidden that thy son, raised from the dead,
Be offered a burnt-offering on the height
Of Carmel! He who gave thy heart's delight,
Twice pitying thee, now bids that it be laid
Upon His altar." But the woman said,
"O, man of God! ne'er would that cruel rite
Be claimed by Him who gave me back my boy.
Some evil spirit has thy ear deceived.
I know that He who pitied when I grieved
And turned the anguish of my heart to joy,
Would not desire such painful sacrifice —
No incense sweet to Him would thence arise."

THE CRITERION OF REVELATION.

II.

" Hast thou the wisdom to determine when
Commands from Heaven are His, and when not so?
How can a heart He trieth if it show
Bold disobedience, ever hope again?"
The prophet spake, but not less boldly then
The woman:— " Well His goodness do I know.
My faith therein no words can overthrow,
Spoken by angels or by holy men.
He tries me by this test? It cannot be
He so delighteth in obedience
That He would break a heart to draw it thence.
No proof thereof would make Him pleased to see
A mother's agony, though hushed her cries,
When yielding up her child for sacrifice."

THE CRITERION OF REVELATION.

III.

ELISHA sped away to Carmel's wild,
  And to the Lord thus prayed with many a tear:
  " Be merciful to her who will not hear
Thy word, though Thou did'st raise to life her child!"
And the Lord answered with reproof though mild:
  " For her thou need'st not my displeasure fear!
  An evil spirit did deceive thine ear.
Now learn of her to be no more beguiled;
For, mindful of the favor to her given,
  She in my goodness hath abiding faith;
  And whatsoe'er of me another saith,
Although the words may seem to come from Heaven,
  She ponders well, and tries it by the test
  Of that which in her heart she findeth best."

www.ingramcontent.com/pod-product-compliance
Lightning Source LLC
Chambersburg PA
CBHW022136160426
43197CB00009B/1310